Toucans

By Sam Dollar

Steadwell Books

Raintree Steck-Vaughn Publishers

A Harcourt Company

Austin · New York

www.steck-vaughn.com

ANIMALS OF THE RAIN FOREST

Published by Raintree Steck-Vaughn Publishers, an imprint of Steck-Vaughn Company.

Library of Congress Cataloging-in-Publication Data
Dollar, Sam.
    Toucans/by Sam Dollar.
        p.cm.--(Animals of the rain forest)
    Includes index.
    ISBN 0-7398-3100-3
    1. Toucans--Juvenile literature. [1. Toucans.] I. Title. II. Series.

Printed in the United States of America
10 9 8 7 6 5 4 3 2 1 LB 02 01 00

Produced by Compass Books

Photo Acknowledgments
Martin Vince, 16, 20, 22, 24 (top and bottom)
Photo Network/Mark Newman, 15
Photophile, 4–5; Anthony Mercieca, 18
Unicorn Stock Photos/Tommy Dodson, 29
Visuals Unlimited/James Beveridge, cover; Tom Ulrich, title
    page, 12; Fritz Pölking, 8; William Grenfell, 11; Inga Spence, 25
Wildlife Conservation Society/Diane Shapiro, 26

Content Consultant
Martin Vince
Assistant Bird Curator
Riverbanks Zoo and Botanical Garden, Columbia, South Carolina

Contents

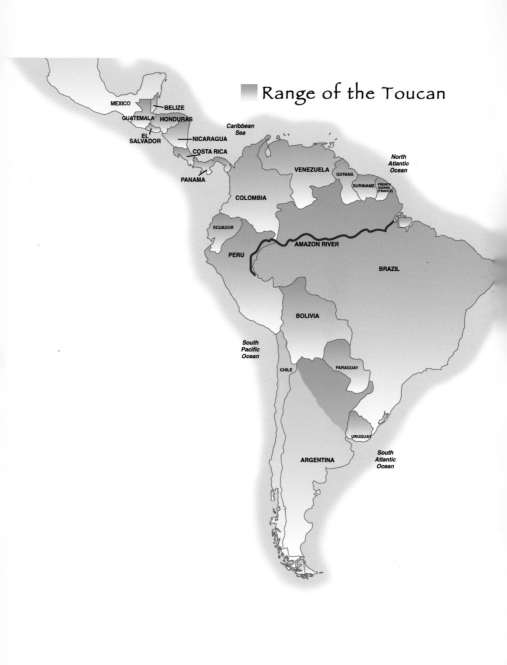

Range of the Toucan

MEXICO
BELIZE
GUATEMALA HONDURAS
EL SALVADOR
NICARAGUA
COSTA RICA
PANAMA

Caribbean Sea

VENEZUELA
GUYANA
SURINAME
FRENCH GUIANA (FRANCE)

North Atlantic Ocean

COLOMBIA

ECUADOR

PERU

AMAZON RIVER

BRAZIL

BOLIVIA

South Pacific Ocean

CHILE
PARAGUAY

URUGUAY

ARGENTINA

South Atlantic Ocean

A Quick Look at Toucans

What do toucans look like?
Toucans are colorful birds
with large bills. An average
toucan bill is about 8 inches
(20 cm) long.

Where do toucans live?
Toucans live in South America
and Central America. They live
in the treetops of rain forests.

What do toucans eat?
Toucans mainly eat fruit. They
sometimes eat insects and
small animals.

Do toucans have any enemies?
Eagles, hawks, ocelots, and snakes eat toucans.
Many animals eat toucan eggs.

This toucan is resting on a branch high in the treetops.

Toucans in the Rain Forest

Toucans are birds that live in South and Central America. They have colorful feathers and large banana-shaped beaks called bills. A toucan's bill can be as long as its body.

Toucans are colorful birds. There are 35 kinds of toucans. Each kind has different colors. They can be white, red, blue, green, black, yellow, and orange.

Many toucans live in Amazonia. This is the world's largest rain forest. It grows around the banks of the Amazon River in South America. It is home to more than 1,600 kinds of birds.

Toucans are an important part of the rain forest. They spit up the seeds from the fruit they eat. New trees grow from the seeds. This helps the rain forest spread to new places.

Toucans travel around the rain forest with other toucans. A group of toucans is called a flock. There are usually between 4 and 12 toucans in a flock. They sleep, eat, and even play together.

Where Toucans Live

Toucans live in most areas of South and Central America. Most kinds of toucans live in lowland rain forest habitats. A habitat is a place where an animal or plant usually lives and grows. It is very warm in the lowlands. But a few kinds of toucans live in mountain forests. It is cooler in the mountains.

Toucans live in the forest canopy about 150 feet (46 km) above the ground. The canopy is a thick area of leaves high up in the treetops. It is like a giant umbrella of leaves and branches.

Toucans rarely leave the forest canopy because all they need is there. Different kinds of fruit grow on the trees. Water collects on leaves and tree branches. Toucans fly or hop to different tree branches to find food and water.

Toucans are heavy birds. They sit on thick branches because thin branches might break.

Toucans sometimes fly to different parts of the rain forest.

Special Body Parts

Toucans have large, brightly colored bills. A toucan's bill might have several patches of different colors on it. This makes the toucan easy to spot.

An average toucan bill is about 8 inches (20 cm) long. But toucans' bills are hollow and very light. The birds use their bills to pick fruit from high branches.

Toucans' feet and legs help them move around the rain forest. Their feet have two claws in the front and two in the back. These claws allow toucans to grip branches. Toucans also have powerful legs. Their strong legs help them hop from branch to branch.

Toucans' wings are short and round. Their wings help toucans keep their balance as they move from tree to tree. Toucans also use their wings to fly to different parts of the rain forest.

Groups of Toucans

Scientists have divided toucans into four main groups. These groups are the Ramphastos, Aracaris, Toucanets, and Mountain Toucans. Each kind of toucan fits into one of these groups.

Toucans in the Ramphastos group are the largest toucans. They have mainly black plumage. Plumage is all of a bird's feathers. Toco toucans belong to the Ramphastos group.

Toucans in the Aracaris group are small and thin. They have smaller bills than the larger Ramphastos toucans. Red-necked aracaris belong to the Aracaris group. They have a bright yellow band across their chests.

Toucans in the Toucanet group often have bright-green plumage. They live in both cool mountain forests and lowland rain forests. Emerald toucanets belong to the Toucanet group. Their bright green plumage gives them camouflage. Camouflage is coloring that blends in with the things around it, such as the green leaves in the canopy.

This large toucan is a member of the Ramphastos group.

Toucans in the Mountain Toucan group live in the Andes Mountains and other South American mountains.

Black-billed mountain toucans belong to the Mountain Toucan group. They have special coloring. They have brown backs and wings and light blue bellies. No other toucan group has this light-blue coloring.

This adult toucan is feeding insects to its young.

Survival

Toucans are omnivores. They eat both animals and plants. Toucans' bills are lighter and not as hard as some other birds. They are not able to crunch hard food well. Like all birds, toucans have no teeth to chew food.

Toucans mainly eat soft fruit. Many different fruits grow all year in the warm rain forest. In the wild, toucans eat about 100 kinds of fruit, such as berries and bananas.

Toucans feed insects and animals to their young to help them grow. These include termites, spiders, and even lizards, snakes, or baby birds.

| This toucan has found a tree with plenty of fruit to eat.

Finding Food and Eating

Toucans use their long bills to grab fruit that is hard to reach. Their bills also have small ridges. These ridges are like the blade of a saw. Toucans use the ridges to cut chunks out of pieces of fruit.

Toucans sometimes eat young birds. They wave their bills around to scare away adult birds from bird nests. Then toucans eat the young birds left alone in the nests.

Toucans swallow their food whole. Getting food to their throats can be hard because their bills are so long. Toucans grab a piece of fruit in their bills. Then they raise their heads up in the air. This makes the fruit slide from the tips of their bills down to their throats.

Escaping Predators

Toucans' plumage helps them hide from predators. Predators hunt and eat other animals. Larger birds, such as eagles and hawks, eat toucans. Colorful feathers help toucans blend in with their surroundings. They can sit still on tree branches and look like flowers.

Predators have a hard time seeing toucans at night. Toucans sleep in a strange way. They turn their heads around backward. They lay their bills over their backs. Then they tip their tails up to cover their bills. They sleep this way so that many toucans can fit on canopy branches. This way of sleeping hides toucans from predators because toucans' bills are hidden in their feathers. Predators do not realize that the sleeping toucans are birds.

A Toucan's Life Cycle

Toucans mate during the warm, rainy season. Males put on a show to attract female toucans. They sing. They fluff up their feathers to show off their colors. They swing their bills up and down.

Bill fencing is often a part of mating. This toucan mating practice was named after the sport of fencing. In fencing, people fight with long, thin swords. In bill fencing, a male toucan uses his bill to hit a female's bill. The female uses her bill to hit him back.

Toucans wave their bills up and down to attract other toucans.

> ⬆ **This toucan is on a branch outside its nest. The nest opening is in the tree.**

Nesting

Toucans search for places to build their nests after they have attracted mates. Making a nest together is an important part of mating.

All toucans build nests high above the ground within holes in trees. Toucan bills are not hard enough to make nesting holes in trees. They must find holes. Small toucans use woodpecker or parrot holes. Large toucans are too big to fit in these holes. Instead, they must use rotten patches in trees.

Males and females work together to make a roomlike nest chamber inside the opening. The chamber must be large enough to hold several eggs. Toucans use their bills to dig out rotten wood or plants. This makes the opening larger.

Females are ready to lay eggs about two weeks after mating. They lay between two and four white eggs.

Protecting the Nest

Predators try to find toucan nests. Eagles, weasels, monkeys, and other animals eat eggs and young toucans. Adult toucans try to hide their nests from predators. They will not fly to their nests if they see predators nearby.

Toucans do not fight to protect the nest if predators find them. They fly away. Toucans would be killed if they tried to fight predators.

Nestlings

Toucan eggs hatch in about 18 days. Newly hatched toucans are called nestlings. Nestlings have short bills and bare red skin. A thick pad of skin around each ankle protects them from the rough floor of the nest chamber.

Nestlings grow slowly. Their eyes stay closed for three weeks. The parents take care of the nestlings while they grow. They feed the nestlings at least five times a day. They keep the nest clean by scooping waste into their bills. They then fly out of the nest and dump the waste. One of the parents sleeps with the nestlings at night. This keeps the nestlings warm.

It takes about seven weeks for nestlings to grow their feathers. The young birds are then called fledglings. The pads on their ankles begin to disappear. Fledglings have short, lightly colored bills. Their bodies are still growing. But fledglings are able to fly.

These newly hatched toucans still have their eyes closed (top). This 13-day-old toucan has no feathers yet (bottom).

▲ **This fledgling has grown some feathers and is able to fly.**

Young toucans are in danger from predators. Fledglings are weak and cannot protect themselves. Adult toucans do not fight to protect them either.

Young toucans usually grow to become healthy adults if they escape predators. Most toucans live about 16 years.

Toucans spend a great deal of time cleaning their feathers. People use toucan feathers to make things.

Living with Toucans

People and toucans have been living together for thousands of years. In Amazonia, toucans have been an important food for people. They also make things out of toucan feathers. Some of the people of Amazonia believe that toucans have special powers.

Today, toucans are popular birds in many parts of the world. People visit North American zoos to see toucans. Some artists paint or draw pictures of toucans. People buy toucan calendars and toucan postcards. A cereal company uses a cartoon toucan on its boxes and in its commercials.

Pet Toucans

Some toucans never live in the wild. People raise toucans to sell to people as pets. Toucans are popular pets. They cannot talk like parrots. But they are smart birds. People can teach them tricks such as rolling over and playing fetch or catch.

Toucans can stay in indoor or outdoor cages. Indoor cages need to be fairly large. Toucans need room to exercise. Outdoor cages are called flights. Flights are much larger than indoor cages. Toucans can fly around in them.

Toucans in Danger

Hunting puts toucans in danger. People hunt toucans for food. Others hunt them for their colorful feathers and bills. People use toucan bills to make medicines.

The main danger to toucans is rain forest destruction. People are cutting down many trees in the rain forest to build homes and farms. Toucans live in the trees of the rain forest. Without the rain forest, toucans cannot live in the wild.

Toucans need rain forest trees to live in the wild.

Glossary

Amazonia (am-uh-ZONE-ee-uh)—the largest rain forest in the world

canopy (KAN-uh-pee)—a thick area of leaves high up in the treetops

fledgling (FLEJ-ling)—a young bird that has just grown its feathers and is able to fly

flight (FLITE)—a large, outdoor bird cage

flock (FLOK)—a group of birds

habitat (HAB-i-tat)—the place where an animal or plant naturally lives and grows

nestlings (NEST-lings)—newly hatched birds

omnivore (OM-nuh-vor)—an animal that eats both animals and plants

plumage (PLOO-mij)—all of a bird's feathers

predator (PRED-uh-tur)—an animal that hunts and eats other animals

Internet Sites and Addresses

Neotropical Bird Club
http://www.neotropicalbirdclub.org/index.html

Riverbanks Zoo and Garden
http://www.riverbanks.org/aig

Toucan.Org
http://www.toucan.org

Emerald Forest Bird Gardens
38420 Dos Cameos Drive
Fallbrook, CA 92028

Rainforest Action Network
221 Pine Street Suite 500
San Francisco, CA 94104

Index